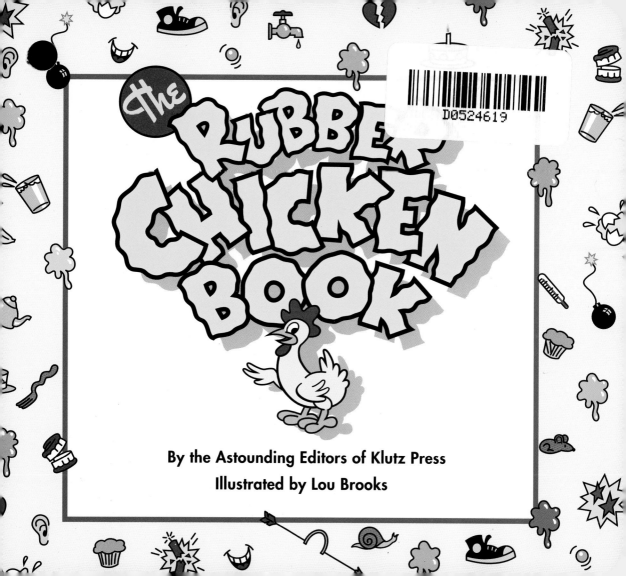

The RUBBER CHICKEN BOOK

By the Astounding Editors of Klutz Press

Illustrated by Lou Brooks

Illustrations: Lou Brooks
Interference throughout:
John Cassidy
Design and Layout:
MaryEllen Podgorski
and Jill Turney
Sourcing and Manufacturing:
Dewitt Durham

Write Us.
Klutz Press is an independent publisher
located in Palo Alto, California and staffed
entirely by real human beings. We
would love to hear your comments
regarding this or any of our other
books. Catalogue available.

Klutz Press
2121 Staunton Court
Palo Alto, CA 94306

ISBN 1-57054-021-7

4 1 5 8 5 7 0 8 8
Book manufactured in Singapore;
Rubber eggs and noisemaker
manufactured in Taiwan.

Did you just pick your nose?

No, I was born

with it.

Ladies and jellyfish, reptiles and crocodiles, I stand before you to sit behind you, to tell you something I know nothing about.

Next Thursday which is Good Friday, we will be having a Women's Meeting. For men only. Absolutely no admission! Plenty of seats—we'll sit on the floor. Tomorrow night, right after breakfast, we'll gather to discuss what color to whitewash the school.

But for now, we have a berrific took for you. Unfortunately, it has been approved for immature audiences only. So put your tray tables and seat backs in a full upright position, stand up, sit down, leave by the side exits and I certainly hope you employ yourselves.

LADIES AND JELLYFISH

SCRAMBLED RUBBER EGGS

Drop the three eggs that came with this book on a hard cement floor. You will note that they bounce and do not break. This is a direct result of the fact that they come from rubber chickens, not normal barnyard chickens.

The advantages of rubber eggs over normal, old-fashioned, breakable eggs are enormous and far too numerous to catalogue in their entirety here. However, here are just a few of them:

Put these three rubber eggs in the egg tray in the fridge. Tomorrow morning, breakfast time, open up the door and take them out. As you carry them toward the frying pan, stumble badly. If you do it right, all of them will come flying out of your hands directly onto whoever else is in the kitchen with you. Gets a terrific response every time.

**HINT:
Always store
eggs in the
fridge. They'll
stay funnier!**

What's green, wears shades and sings? Elvis Parsely.

Or, take one of them out of the fridge and announce that you have a neat idea. You need a volunteer. But don't wait for any, just slip the egg into someone's pocket, say a few magic words and whap it once. Hysterical.

Or, you might just want to secretly sit on them all sometime when you're at a meal. Then, a little later, start acting very strange. Cross your eyes, make a lot of clucking noises and finally stand up. Point excitedly at your seat cushion. ("OMYGOSH! I HAD NO IDEA! THREE OF THEM! I DON'T KNOW IF I'M READY! I'M SO EXCITED!!") Then, in a clumsy frenzy, pick them all up and drop them on someone's lap.

Or, when fancy guests are over, come staggering into the room with an egg balanced over one eye (throw your head way back). Accompany yourself with circus music and weave all over the room. Then if it hasn't fallen off, remove it, take a deep bow and flip it to your guest (the egg, not your head).

We will leave the three million other possibilities as a homework assignment.

Just remember, immaturity is the key!

Why did the lady blush when she walked past the chicken coop?

Because she heard fowl language.

Here are the second place finishers in our knock-knock joke section. Not as good as the interrupting cow, but there's only room at the top for one.

Knock-knock.
Who's there?
Little old lady.
Little old lady who?
I didn't know you
could yodel.

Knock-knock.
Who's there?
Dwayne.
Dwayne who?
Dwayne the bathtub.
I'm dwowning.

Knock-knock.
Who's there?
Juan.
Juan who?
Juan, two, three, four,
when you gonna
open the door?

Knock-knock.
Who's there?
Hooo.
Hooo who?
What are you, an owl?

Knock-knock.
Who's there?
Accordian.
Accordian who?
Accordian to the paper,
it's going to snow today.

Knock-knock.
Who's there?
Cargo.
Cargo who?
Cargo 'beep, beep'.

Knock-knock.
Who's there?
Doris.
Doris who?
Doris closed, that's why
I knocked!

Knock-knock.
Who's there?
Cows.
Cows who?
Cows go 'moo',
not 'who'.

Knock-knock.
Who's there?
Freddie.
Freddie who?
Freddie or not,
here I come

Knock-knock.
Who's there?
Dishwasher.
Dishwasher who?
Dishwasher the way I
spoke before I had
false teeth.

Knock-knock.
Who's there?
Hatch.
Hatch who?
Gesundheit.

Knock-knock.
Who's there?
Alex.
Alex who?
Alexplain later.

Knock-knock.
Who's there?
Oswald.
Oswald who?
Oswald my gum.

What does a 200 lb. mouse say? "Here, kitty, kitty, kitty . . ."

7

HOW TO TURN A BAD JOKE INTO A GREAT SKIT

A ny joke, no matter how lame, can be massively improved if you act it out. How to do that? First, break your joke up into roles (*"You be the duck, I'll be the lady with the big hat . . ."*).

Then you'll need a stage. Move a piece of furniture around. It almost doesn't matter where, as long as the room looks different—that makes it special.

When you're ready to begin, step center stage and hold a hand towel in front of your face while the crowd* quiets down. Then

GORILLA

slowly, very slowly, gather it up into your hands revealing your face. Then announce the skit and set the scene (". . . this lady was walking down the street when a duck came up and said . . .").

If you need a tree, building, fire hydrant, mountain or whatever, just get Dad or someone up on stage, hang a sign on him ("tree") and tell him not to move no matter what. And don't let your audience just sit there! Tell them to hoot and holler for the good guys, and hiss and boo for the bad guys. Or just tell them to stomp their feet and clap.

* "Crowd" usually means one parent and the dog

Most important! When you reach the end of the skit don't just stand there or walk off—take a huge bo

GOTTA GO WEE
A VERY OLD SKIT FOR TWO

Father and son are at a football game. Son is sitting down looking very uncomfortable. Dad is up on his feet, jumping and shouting. Son tugs on father's shirt.

"Dad, I gotta go wee."

"Not now, Henry. Later." Starts jumping and cheering again.

"Daaaaddddd! I gotta go wee!"

"Henry, I said later!"

This goes on for another round or two with Henry getting more and more insistent. Finally . . .

"DAAAAAAADDDDD! I GOTTA GO WEEEEE!"

"Oh, all right, Henry."

Henry jumps up and shouts

"WEEEEEEEEEE!"

What do you give a seasick elephant? Plenty of room.

9

GRANNY GETS A LITTLE GROSS

A GROUP SKIT, OR A ONE-PERSON STORY

The kids have stopped at Granny's on Halloween and they're standing on the porch. She has a bowl of peanuts she's passing around.

As the last kid is eating the last one, he suddenly stops and says, "Gee, Granny, I ate the last peanut. I should have asked if you wanted any . . ."

(Granny has false teeth, so she speaks with a kind of lisp.)

"Oh, that's alright, thweetie. Those were M&Ms and eber since I lost my weal teeth, all I've been able to do ith thuck off the chocolate anyway."

Q: What does a mobster buried in cement soon become? A: A hardened criminal.

THE TWO FISHERMEN AND THE BUG

A TWO-PERSON SKIT

Two fishermen are in a small boat. Fisherman #1 is casting away minding his own business. Then he stops and swats a mosquito on his arm and says "Dang bugs!"

Fisherman #2 is casting happily away. He looks over at the other fisherman and suddenly stops casting. He looks intently at the forehead of the other fisherman. Slowly he sets down his fishing rod, pulls his hand back and whispers to his friend . . .

"Don't move."

KA-WHAM!

He slaps him on the forehead. The other fisherman is practically knocked out of the boat. But he staggers back up, holding his head and says . . ."Did you get him?"

Fisherman #2 (innocently): "Get what?"

11

DAD BUYS HIS UNDERWEAR

A Skit

You need three kids and a dad, or somebody like a dad, in the audience.

One kid is a department store clerk. The other two are customers.

The first kid (customer) goes up to the department store clerk with a handful of underwear.

Customer: "I'd like seven pair of underwear, please."

Clerk: "Gee that seems like quite a few. Why seven?"

Customer: "Oh, you know. Monday, Tuesday, Wednesday . . ."

The clerk nods and rings up the sale. Immediately, a second kid goes up and does the same thing. Seven pair of underwear. The clerk says the same thing, and the second kid gives the same answer as the first.

Finally, Dad is grabbed unsuspecting from the audience and given a handful of underwear and told to go up to the clerk to ask to buy twelve pair of underwear.

After he does that, the clerk says, "Gee, twelve pair of underwear, that seems like an awful lot. Why twelve?"

Before Dad can say anything, the other two kids holler out,
"Oh, you know. January, February, March . . ."

AND IF YOU LIKED THAT ONE . . .
(Another underwear skit)

You only need one kid for this one. It's a classic.

The kid is a salesperson on TV. She's selling laundry soap. If you have a cardboard box you can cut out, get inside of and turn into a TV, that would be perfect, but it's not totally necessary. What is necessary is a handful of underwear. One of them should be Dad's (or somebody like Dad).

The salesperson is on TV singing a little song as she scrubs the first pair of underwear in a pretend bucket of water.

"Wishy washy wishy washy

New Blue Cheer

Wishy washy wishy washy

Ever so clear,

Put 'em to your nose,

She puts the pair to her nose and takes a deep sniff, . . .

. . . then she smiles and while she puts it away, she says,

Smells like a rose."

She takes the second pair of underwear and goes through the whole thing again. When she gets to the last line ("Smells like a rose.") she gives another big smile and puts the underwear aside.

Now for the third pair. It should have a sign stuck to it that says something like "Dad's Underwear." The happy salesperson goes through everything again, rubbing the underwear up and down in the pretend bucket and singing her little song. Then, she gets to the part where she takes the big sniff and says

Put it to your nose . . ."

There's a long pause . . .

. . . and she goes right back to the top of her little song and starts scrubbing them again

"Wishy washy wishy washy

New Blue Cheer . . ."

13

WHO NEEDS TEN FINGERS? ●
(HOW TO GET RID OF THAT EXTRA ONE)

Here's a little math quiz you can give your friends.

Hold up one hand and ask them to count the fingers.

If they're able to do that, hold up the other and ask them to try again. If they get it right the second time, go for the final exam.

Lace your fingers together as shown, with the ring finger hiding. Practice by yourself a minute or two so you don't fumble and stumble or you'll lose the whole effect.

Then, ask them to count both hands together.

Answer: Nine.
(Isn't higher math amazing?)

WIGGLE WH?CH FINGER

1 Get your victim to cross his wrists and put his hands together, palm to palm, but with pinkies up.

2 Then have him interlace his fingers.

3 While his fingers are still interlaced, have your victim bring his hands up towards his chin.

4 Now, point at one of the fingers (<u>but do not touch</u>) and tell your victim to try to wiggle it. Not easy.

Weird GHOST ARMS

Stand in a doorway and press the backs of your hands against the doorjam as shown. Do it hard and do it for 60 <u>slow</u> seconds. Count out loud. As you count, press harder and harder until you're really hurting. This is the fun part.

At the count of 60, step forward and totally relax your arms. They will float upwards all on their own.

Q: What's this?

.... A: A clam with buck teeth.

THE
WIDE MOUTHED FROG

A JOKE FOR ONE
OR A SKIT FOR MORE

We're in a swamp and watching a type of frog—called the Wide Mouthed Frog—as he hops around meeting some of his forest friends and surveying their eating habits.

Wide Mouthed Frog spots a raccoon. "Hey, Mr. Raccoon, what do you eat for dinner?" Only he doesn't say it that way. Wide mouthed frogs keep their mouths wide open all the time, so it sounds like "Heeey, Mr. Racoooon, whaaaat dooooo yoooou eeeat foooor dinner?"

Raccoon: "Oh, bugs, fish, slimy little things. Stuff like that."

WMF says "Thaaaaank yooooou," and hops on until he sees a deer, never closing his mouth.

WMF: "Heeeey, Mr. Deeeeeeer, whaaaaaaaat dooooo yooooooooou eeeeeeeat foooooooor dinner?"

Deer: "Mostly trees, grass, shrubs . . . green stuff."

WMF says "Thaaaaaaank yooooooou," and hops on until he sees an alligator.

WHF: "Heeeey, Mr. Aligaaaaatoooor, whaaaaaaaat dooooo yooooooooou eaaaaaaat foooooooor dinner?"

Alligator: "Wide mouthed frogs, mostly."

WMF slams his mouth shut and says, through tightly pursed lips . . .

"OH. THANK YOU."

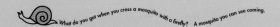 What do you get when you cross a mosquito with a firefly? A mosquito you can see coming.

17

THE FABULOUS
NO-BRAIN TWO-WORD
Romantic Skit

If you can't remember lines to save your life, but you hunger for stardom, this could be your ticket.

You'll need a friend. If you're a boy, your friend should be a girl. If you're a girl, your friend should be a boy.

Step One: Dress in each other's clothes.

OK, you can skip this part if it's too embarassing. But it can make this a very special theatrical experience if you do.

Step Two: We'll make you the girl in guy's clothes. The curtain rises on the two of you walking into the room. A table with two chairs is already there. (To make the curtain rise, just say "Curtain." Works every time.)

Step Three: You walk to the table and pull out the chair for your friend. You sit down and start a little chitchat. The chitchat gets a little friendlier. You exchange a few romantic glances. Then you reach over for your friend's hand and start to bring it up for a kiss.

But your friend pulls it back, modestly. You try again. No luck. Your friend starts to object. You try again. Your friend gets huffy, stands up and stomps out of the room. End of story and curtain.

It's a simple story, but the fun part is this: Each character says only one word the whole time. The boy says "Judy" and the girl says "Bob."

The trick is to say the same word over and over and change it enough so that the story is told with only body movements and a changing tone of voice. So it goes like this . . . "Bob!" "Judy!" "Bob!!!" "Juuuudy!!!" "Booooooob!!!!" "Judy?" "Bob?" "Judy!!!?" "Bob!!!?" and so on and so forth. Easy lines to memorize; all it takes is a lot of over-acting.

Incidentally, you shouldn't use "Bob" and "Judy." Use your parents' names, or some other couple who'd appreciate the attention.

19

FOLLOW THE

BOUNCING CUPCAKE

Gentle reader, please learn this trick. After you've bounced a cupcake sky-high off the floor, your life will be enriched. Trust us.

Sit down at a table. Grab something and throw it hard to the ground right at your feet. Give it a good wind-up and really let fly!

Pretend you're walking a friend through your house and stop in front of a portrait on the wall. You tell your friend: "Brothers and sisters have I none, but that person's father is my father's son." Whose picture are you looking at?

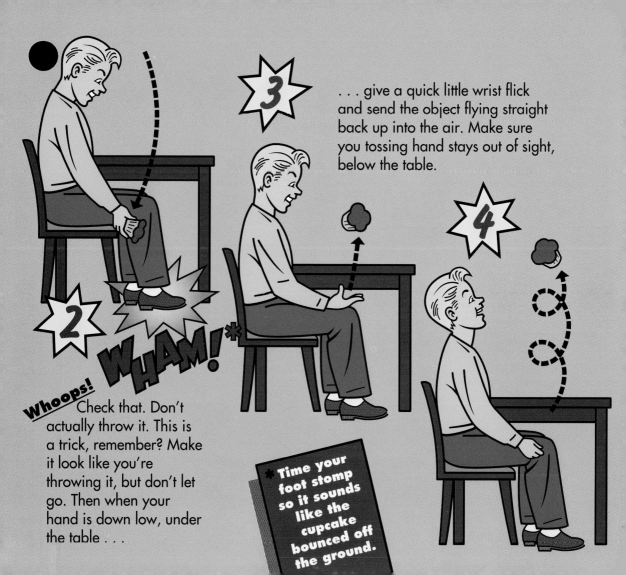

BREAK YOUR NOSE

Put your hands over your nose like this. Make a horrible face and slowly (very slowly) bend your nose more and more until you hear a loud

SNAP! POP!

. . . the sound of a human nose breaking. Remove your hands and smile winningly. You can get the all-important sound effects either by really breaking your nose, which we don't recommend, or by catching your thumb-nail just under your front tooth and then, at just the right moment, popping it off as loudly as you can.

GRASS SHRIEKING

Hold a blade of grass as shown between your thumbs. Press it to your mouth and blow through it hard. If you're lucky, and hold the grass tight, you will create a very loud and irritating noise.

Helpful hint: Ask the kid next to you if you're having trouble, or maybe even your parent. Grass shrieking has been around a while.

WELL, NO WONDER MY FOOT WAS KILLING ME

Stick a tennis ball just inside your pocket so it's a quick move to get it out, but still out of sight. Complain to your friend about something in your shoe and then turn sideways to her and pull off the shoe. As you remove the shoe, grab the tennis ball and pop it into the shoe (watch your angles and you can get away with this). Then turn and shake out the shoe.

STICK A NEEDLE THROUGH YOUR NOSE

Just kidding. PRETEND to stick an invisible needle and thread through your lip. Then PRETEND to pull it through your nose. Then PRETEND to pull on it. And then REALLY sneer. If your timing is right, it looks disgustingly great.

AND IF YOU LIKED THAT ONE...

Take the same pretend needle and thread and stick it through each of your fingers in turn. Don't forget to wince every time you stick it through. Then pretend to tug on the thread and pull all your fingers together, until your fingers are sewn shut. Very nice effect.

HOW TO FREAK OUT JUST ABOUT ANYBODY

The next time you see a magazine cover with a photograph of some big celebrity's face on the cover, cut out a little hole in the mouth, then hold the picture up over your face and stick your tongue through the hole. Then walk around and watch the people run screaming from the room.

WATER ON THE BRAIN

Empty a cup of water into your mouth, fake the swallow and then lean your head way over. "Pour" the empty cup into your ear and straighten up. Cross your eyes and suddenly spit out the water. (We tried this on an audience of single-celled animals once. They got it and loved it.)

NYAH!

TIME

THE AMAZING MUSIC MACHINE● THINGAMAPERSON

Two people are needed for this skit. One to be the amazing music machine, the other to be the operator.

The music machine person stands at attention and never says a word.

The operator steps up and pushes on her belly button. She goes "squonk." He presses on her nose. She goes "ahchoo."

He rotates her arm. She goes "thweepathweepa-thweepa." He pulls on her ear. She goes "BAM BAM BAM!" He raps on top of her head. She goes "Abraca-dooodoo!"

No matter where he pinches, pokes, tweaks, turns, thumps or touches . . . the Amazing Music Machine Thingama-person has a sound effect. Of course, the problem is when the operator starts repeating, the Amazing Music Machine Thingama-person has to remember what sounds come from where.

For the GRAND FINALE

The operator should play "Twinkle Twinkle Little Star" on the Amazing Music Machine Thingamaperson by poking and prodding at all the appropriate places while the music machine person performs all her sound effects to the tune.

(**Note:** This has been extensively tested at slumber parties and found to be <u>highly</u> entertaining.)

BABYSITTER BUMPER CARS

You'll need a couple of people for this one. A babysitter would be perfect if you have one. The idea is simple: Somebody (say the babysitter) has to close his eyes, no cheating. The other person (or people) then shouts out directions ("Go left!" "Go right!" "Stop" "Back up!"). The goal is to get the "blinded" one all the way through the house without bumping into anything.

From a short-legged cow. How do you get dragon milk?

Hungry man at a restaurant to waiter: "I guess I'll have whatever that fellow over there is having." Waiter, after hesitating: "Okay, but I don't think he's going to be very happy about it." What's green, wears a mask, and

What do you get when you cross a dog with a lion? A nervous mailman.

Customer: Have you ever hunted bear? New Customer: No, but I've gone fishing in short shorts.

rides a horse? The Lone Pickle.

Hunting Guide to New

PSYCHIC SILVERWARE POWERS

With nothing but the power of your astonishing psycho-kinetic mental powers—and your lying tongue—you will be able to staighten a bent fork in front of your audience's disbelieving eyes.

You're sitting at the table with your family and friends. Grab a fork and (secretly) hold it and a dime in both hands as shown in The Set Up. Place the tines against the edge of the table and bring everyone's attention to it. Grunt and groan while you fake-bend it. Show a sliver of dime at the top (looks like the top of the fork) and this fake-bend looks terrific. Before Mom can even holler at you, tell everyone to be totally silent. Close your eyes, hold your breath, and concentrate on the fork (still concealed in your hand). Then, with a flourish, open your hands.
Normal fork!
No bend!

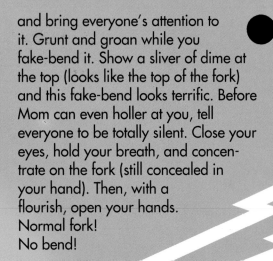

THE SET UP

dime ➔

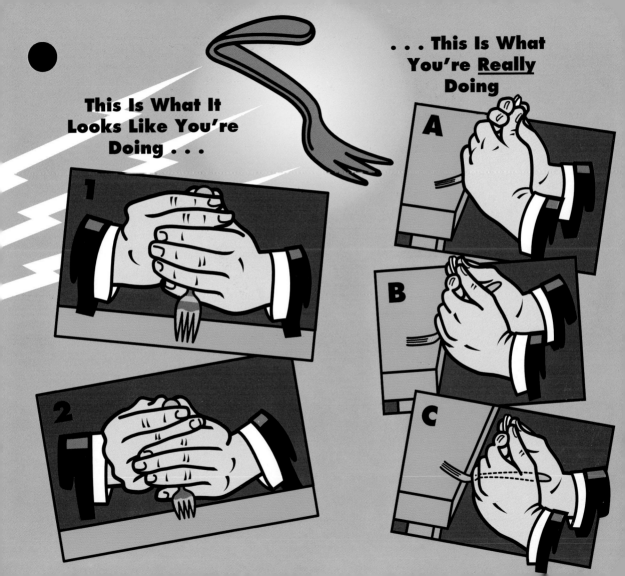

SICK JOKES: THE DOCTOR AND HER PATIENT

You can either tell these jokes all by yourself, or get a friend to lie down on a table and be the patient—instant skit.

Mother (*rushing up to doctor*): "Doctor, Doctor, I need to see my son! He's been run over by a steamroller!"

Doctor: "Oh, yes. The steamroller victim. You'll find him in rooms 103, 104, and 105.

Patient: Doc, after you operate on my hands, will I be able to play the piano?
Doctor: Of course.
Patient: That's wonderful. I've always wanted to play the piano.

Doctor: Mr. Jones, has anyone taken your temperature today?
Patient: No. I didn't even know it was missing.

Patient: Doctor, whenever my foot falls asleep, it wakes me up.
Doctor: How can your foot falling asleep wake you up?
Patient: It snores.

Doctor: (*holding up the eye chart*): Can you read this line?
Patient: 10-Q 10-Q 10-Q
Doctor: You're very welcome.

Patient: Doctor, I'm having a terrible memory problem.
Doctor: How long have you been having this problem?
Patient: Problem? What problem?

Doctor: Have your eyes been checked lately?
Patient: No, they've always been plain brown.

AN EXTREMELY IMMATURE HIGH SCHOOL TRICK WITH  A QUARTER

When you're sitting down with some friends, take out a quarter and toss it around then, just for kicks, slowly roll it down the middle of your face—from the top of your forehead to your chin. Close your eyes and tell them how weird it feels, kind of zen-like. If they scoff, pull out another quarter and let them try.

As they do, a pencil line track will be left where the quarter rolled over their face. Why? Simple. Because you're immature and rubbed a pencil lead against the edge of that quarter before the whole thing started.

What do you get if you cross a lake with a leaky boat?

About half-way.

What was the last thing to enter the bug's mind as he hit the windshield?

His back legs.

Why did Robin Hood steal from the rich?

They're the only ones with the money.

PLUMBER'S FIELD GOAL

Set a clean plumber's helper on the floor about two feet in front of a door with a finish that can stand a little abuse. Back off one step. Take a deep breath, then take one short step—and kick a field goal. Your toe should hit very low on the rubber part (not the stick). Your goal is to stick the thing to the door. This won't happen the first time. If it did, it wouldn't be so special. But, after just a few minutes of practice . . .

BAM!

KICK HERE!

29

MIND IF I SPRAY HAND LOTION ALL OVER YOU!

Keep your eye out for a plastic lotion bottle that has a squirt top. When it's empty, grab it and rinse it out very carefully. Then let it dry and stick a 3- or 4- foot length of white string into the bottle. Thread one end through the squirt top but don't let any of it show from the outside.

Then, the next time you're in the bathroom with somebody, pick up the lotion bottle and ask them if they'd like a little hand lotion squirted all over them. Point the bottle at their chest and give it a good squeeze and the string will come flying out. Gets a great reaction every time.

Helpful Tip: If you tie a little knot on the end of the string, the end won't come out. Then you can pull it back into the bottle and be instantly ready for the next victim.

HOW TO RUIN THE WALLS

This is a terrific little item, buried here in the underbrush. You'll need a sheet of white paper. Fold it in half and tear a small piece out of it. Unfold the little piece and you'll have a small piece of torn paper. Not too exciting. But keep reading, it gets better.

LICK THE BACK

Lick all over the top half of the piece and stick it to the wallpaper, or maybe the cover of some expensive coffee table book.

BEAM ME UP, SCOTTIE!

BY O.U. DoGG

Smooth it out carefully so it looks for all the world like a tear. Then, when Mom or someone is in the room, not paying too much attention, rip a piece of paper under the table (sound effects), and say something like "Whoops!" Show her the torn cover or wallpaper and talk about what an unfortunate accident it was and all that.

Then, for the punchline, rub your hand over the tear and mumble some hocus pocus as you invisibly wad up the piece in your hand. Remove the hand and Presto! Back to normal!

Try this! It works a lot better than you think it will. **31**

SURGERY FOR THE COMPLETE KLUTZ

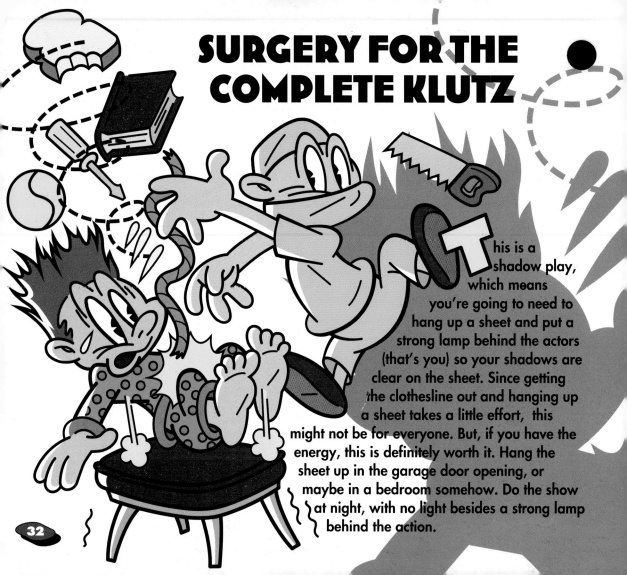

This is a shadow play, which means you're going to need to hang up a sheet and put a strong lamp behind the actors (that's you) so your shadows are clear on the sheet. Since getting the clothesline out and hanging up a sheet takes a little effort, this might not be for everyone. But, if you have the energy, this is definitely worth it. Hang the sheet up in the garage door opening, or maybe in a bedroom somehow. Do the show at night, with no light besides a strong lamp behind the action.

The plot? Mad doctor operates on patient and pulls out all sorts of strange things from inside his or her body, looking for an elusive gallstone.

The patient lies on a table complaining of stomach aches. Doctor comes in with saw (or at least something whose shadow looks like a saw) and proceeds to operate. Then doctor reaches "into" the body and starts pulling out all sorts of bizarre things . . . books, silverware, sticks, car keys, rake, etc. A long piece of rope can be the intestine, a balled T-shirt the stomach. Doctor should be talking all the time about what a disgusting mess all of this is, while he or she tosses all the stuff onto the floor.

Whenever patient complains about something, the doctor just tells the patient to stop whining, he's a professional and knows what he's doing.

All the props should be by the patient's side, so to the audience, they look as if they come from the patient's innards.

To wrap the skit up, the doctor should pull out a football or basketball (with great effort) and announce that the problem gallstone has been found. Act as if it's extremely heavy (grunt and groan). Then, with enormous effort, heave it over the sheet into the audience . . . then come out and take a bow.

Doctor: Mr. Jones, I've looked at your charts and I'm afraid your condition is extremely serious. I think, if you have any last requests to make, anyone you'd like to speak with, now would be the time to do that.

Patient (in a very sick, whispery voice): Yes, Doctor, I do have one request. There is someone I'd like to speak with. **Doctor** (leaning closer): Who is that? **Patient:** I . . . would . . . like . . . to . . . speak . . . with . . . another . . . . doctor.

ORANGE PEEL MONSTER TEETH:

Slice an orange into quarters, peel off the skin from one of them and insert into mouth. For that extra special look, cut monster teeth into it first.

CHERRY STEM KNOTTING:

How many of you out there think it is possible to tie a cherry stem into a knot in your mouth? Tongue power only? No hands?
Answer: You betcha. Don't believe us, though. Try it yourself.

DINNER TIME IS FUN TIME

BODY GRAPES: Secretly put a grape into your ear. (You read that right. Into your ear.) Tell everyone you've been having this weird problem with your food recently, and, while they're watching, pop a grape into your mouth. Fake like you're swallowing it whole, then lean your head over and whap it a couple of times on the side (like you were trying to clear water out of your ear). Out pops the grape onto the floor. ("Weird, huh? Do you think I should see a doctor?")

SPOON HORSESHOES

Nothing like a quick game of competitive Spoon Horseshoes to shorten a tedious wait at a restaurant table

WHAP HERE!

Three points if it goes into glass. (WARNING: This is far from easy.)

PAPER CUP HONK MACHINE

knot

paper cup (or plastic)

white string, at least 12 inches long

With a wet sponge (or wet paper towel), pull down firmly on the string. It makes a loud squonking noise, exactly like a duck with a bad cold.

TOMATO GOOSH MONSTER:

This is an item of genius. Cut a little happy face in a cherry tomato, show it around, and then squeeze it from behind, gooshing all the innards out of the eyes and mouth. Charming.

THE SQUEAK ATTACK

squeeze the squeaker. Act shocked and surprised (and don't reveal the squeaker!).

Or try this: At the dinner table, reach over to the rolls and poke at one of them. A squeaking noise emerges from it. Look confused. Poke again. It squeaks again. Jump out of your chair and babble about spirits in the rolls.

Or how about this: Put a finger in your ear and root around for some lovely ear wax. It's a nasty habit, but it's REALLY disgusting when you add a lot of squeaking noise.

We could go on forever like this. Poke at anything with a squeaker in your hand and the world around you becomes a little weirder.

I f you grab and firmly squeeze the three rubber eggs while they are still in the red bag that came attached to this book, you will note that they emit a squeaking noise.

Actually, this is an illusion. The actual squeaking is done by a terrific little squeaker unit that is also in the bag. Why is there a terrific little squeaker unit in this bag? Because we are immature and there are a whole lot of immature things you can do with this unit.

For example: Hold it in your hand (secretly) and push on someone's nose while you (invisibly)

SQUAWK

Remember the only rule though, NEVER REVEAL YOUR SECRET SQUEAKER!

A COUPLE OF LOVELY PUSH BUTTON TELEPHONE TUNES

Call a friend and perform the following musical compositions (and see if they can "Name That Tune!").

TWINKLE, TWINKLE, LITTLE STAR

1 1 9 9 0 0 9
Twin- kle, twin- kle, lit-tle star

STRANGERS IN THE NIGHT

4 8 8 4 8 4 8 6 8 4
Stran- gers in the night, ex- chang- ing glan- ces

HAPPY BIRTHDAY

4 4 2 4 # 8 1 1 2 1 9 8
Hap- py birth- day to you, Hap- py birth- day to you

AMERICA

5 5 6 1 5 9
My coun- try, 'tis of thee,

0 0 8 0 8 4
Sweet land of li- ber- ty,

8 4 2 4
Of thee I sing

First Roman: What time is it? Second Roman: Half past VII

If athletes get athlete's foot, what do astronauts get? Mistletoe.

What happens when the human body is submerged in water? The telephone rings.

What do you get if you cross a porcupine with a skunk? A smelly pincushion.

Warning: If you don't call someone up BEFORE you play your song, you'll be doing something known as "dialing the telephone" and you will probably get very expensively connected to someone in southern Mongolia.

ONE-KID REMOTE CONTROL SKITS

Not everyone has the nerve to get up in front of an audience (even if it's just Mom and Dad) and put on a one-kid show, but if you've got that kind of star-struck style, have we got something for you.

First Step! Give your audience an invisible "remote control" and tell them they can control the action on stage by pushing the buttons—fast forward, backwards, or super slo-mo. ("Just push the button and announce your selection.")

Then do one (or all) of the following impressions.

1 Stand in front of your audience and announce that you are a bug, flying around a highway. Then put out your arms and go buzzzzing around for a few moments. Suddenly, SPLATT! an ugly windshield end. Look splatted for a moment, then slump slowly to the ground.

2 Here's a small variation on the same theme. Get down on your hands and knees and announce you are a turtle crossing a highway. Crawl very slowly across the room while making all kinds of diesel truck sounds. Don't look either way, and don't change your crawl speed. At the last instant, get squooshed.

3 Stand up tall and announce you are a nail getting hammered. Then make the right kinds of sound effects and slowly— one bang at a time—crouch down to the ground. At the last instant, fall and lay very flat (the "bent nail look").

4 Announce you are a washer with an off-balance load going into the spin cycle. Then spin around and around, more and more wobbly, until you fall over. Don't forget all the sound effects.

You have to be ready at any moment to go into fast forward, reverse or slo-mo on any of these. So stay flexible.

39

Ladies and Gentlemen...

THE CHINNIKINS

This is a skit that goes under the category of Very VERY Strange. Unless you have incredible stage fever, you'll need to do this with at least one friend, and maybe two or three.

Cover your eyes with a t-shirt. Then lie down on a table and hang your head over the edge. Get someone to use washable markers to draw upside-down eyes on your chin. Throw a blanket over your whole body, including your head. Then bring in the audience. You'll need an MC to announce your act (*"Ladies and Gentlemen . . . An amazing new act . . . Just in from the Coast . . . THE CHINNIKINS!"*). Then your MC should put on an old rock n' roll hit and pull back the blanket enough to reveal just your heads as you lip synch along with the music.

Although this may sound funny, it's nothing compared to what it looks like. Excellent slumber party fare.

PEA BURBLING

This little item is flat-out incredible. It can be your route to a better life! More friends! Higher pay!

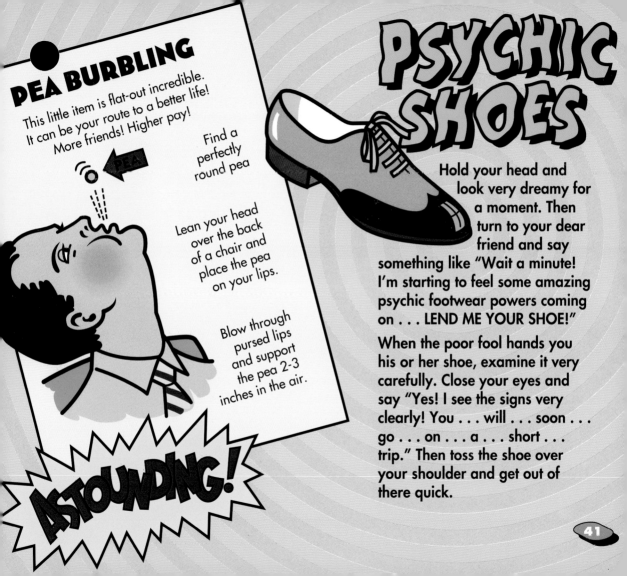

Find a perfectly round pea

← PEA

Lean your head over the back of a chair and place the pea on your lips.

Blow through pursed lips and support the pea 2-3 inches in the air.

ASTOUNDING!

PSYCHIC SHOES

Hold your head and look very dreamy for a moment. Then turn to your dear friend and say something like "Wait a minute! I'm starting to feel some amazing psychic footwear powers coming on . . . LEND ME YOUR SHOE!"

When the poor fool hands you his or her shoe, examine it very carefully. Close your eyes and say "Yes! I see the signs very clearly! You . . . will . . . soon . . . go . . . on . . . a . . . short . . . trip." Then toss the shoe over your shoulder and get out of there quick.

THE INCREDIBLE ANTI-GRAVITY ROPE

Hold a piece of rope or string (maybe a foot or two) vertically in both hands. Show that it is a completely normal string or rope. Explain to your audience: "Please do not breathe for the following demonstration because it depends on a complete absence of any air currents whatsoever."

Wait while everyone holds their breath, then launch into a very scientific speech about gravity and atomic particles and black holes and stuff like that. Glare if anyone has to take a breath. Finally, explain that you are going to remove your hand and yet the rope will remain in the vertical position. Get set, drumroll, and remove your bottom hand. YA GOTTA LOVE IT!

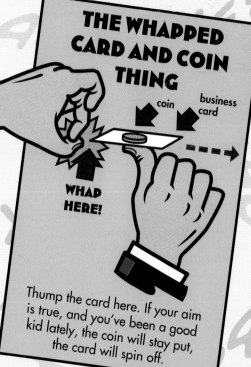

THE WHAPPED CARD AND COIN THING

coin

business card

WHAP HERE!

Thump the card here. If your aim is true, and you've been a good kid lately, the coin will stay put, the card will spin off.

THE BANANA BANDANA

ONE OF THE TOP THREE SUMMER CAMP SKITS OF ALL TIME

Two players are needed. For props, a bandana or handkerchief, and a ripe banana.

You don't have to memorize any lines to do this skit (thank heavens!). Just read it through, get the idea, and then make up your own lines all the way.

A narrator should explain this part: The scene opens on two kids on the phone trying to do their homework. The assignment is an arts and crafts kind of thing—fold a bandana in a special way to make a hat.

Only there's a problem. The second kid wasn't at school today, so she's a little confused about the whole thing. When the first kid says "bandana", she thinks

he said "banana". So she's holding a <u>banana</u> in her hand, and he's holding a <u>bandana</u>. It's one of those mistaken identity things.

Then he starts giving instructions like . . . "First, fold it in half. Then halves again. One more time. Then open it back up, smooth it all down, bring in the edges and re-fold it at the crease."

Naturally, she's a little grossed out by all this, and she makes him repeat everything, but homework is homework—and she keeps plugging away.

Until the last instruction . . . "Now put it on your head." she makes him repeat that three times—but she finally takes the whole disgusting mess and puts it on her head.

What's yellow and goes slam, slam, slam, slam? A 4-door banana.

THE ELECTRIFIED CAP TRICK

This is a perfect example of how a small piece of bald trickery can be made into an awe-inspiring fraud with nothing but the skillful use of your lying tongue.

You'll need one of those pens that look like this. Sorry, no substitions allowed. The cap has to be tapered.

Wet your fingers and pull the cap off the pen. Hold it an inch or two away from the point and squeeze the cap until it squirts out like a watermelon seed.

If you aimed right, it will zing—snap!—onto the pen. Otherwise it will just go flying off into the blue. Practice your aim.

So what? . . . you're saying.

Q: What's this? . . . . A: Tennis ball (factory reject).

46

● Bring in an innocent bystander. Show them the pen and begin a very

L...O...N...G...

explanation of high-voltage, ballpoint pen electrostatics.

Rub the cap against the pen as you talk about the enormous negative charge that is being built up in the cap, at the same time a similar, yet positive, charge is

Warn your audience about trying this in the bathtub, due to the existence of potentially life threatening voltages . . . blah, blah, blah.

being created in your body . . .

When you've finally finished your scientific discourse, make them watch very carefully as you squeeze the cap and send it zipping back onto the pen. Of course, that's not what it looks like. After all your explanation, it will look like an amazing act of atomic-powered electrostatic attraction. Right. Now hand it over and let them try. Rub as they might, it won't work. The cap will not zing back onto the pen. So look at their feet. Maybe their shoes have rubber soles. That's bad, since it insulates them from the floor.

So have them take off their shoes and try again.

Still won't work?

Get them to stand on one foot, or stand on a chair (or both!) so they reduce their grounding. Maybe they should jump at the instant they release the cap . . . ?

A HAPPY ENDING STORY ABOUT A AND A LOAN

(A SKIT FOR A GROUP, OR A JOKE FOR ONE)

A frog was going down to his bank to borrow money for fixing up his lily pad. When he hopped up to the first teller, though, and explained what he wanted, she had a problem:

Teller: I'm sorry Mr. Frog, but if we give you any money, we're going to want something of yours to keep here. Just to make sure you don't run off with the cash. It has to be something valuable, we call it "collateral."

Frog reaches into his pocket and nervously reveals a souvenir his mother had once brought back to him from a trip.

The teller looks over the counter at it: "You've got to be kidding! That little knick-knack! It's worthless. Get lost!"

So the frog tries the next teller and gets exactly the same response when he shows his souvenir. ("That little knick-knack thing! You want us to keep THAT while you have OUR money! Forget it!")

As a last resort, the frog hops up the stairs to the bank president's office. He goes up to the door—it says "Patricia Black, Bank President" on it. He butts his way in and finds himself standing in front of a huge desk with a fierce-looking lady behind it.

Patricia Black: "What do YOU want?"

Nervously, carefully, the frog explains the whole thing again. And then, when she demands to see his collateral, he nervously, carefully pulls out his little knick-knack. Patricia Black stares unbelieving down at it.

Patricia Black: "WHAT is THAT?!"

Just then the shutters blow open, the skies darken and a huge voice booms down . . .

IT'S A KNICK-KNACK, PATTY BLACK! GIVE THE FROG A LOAN!

Did you hear about the two monacles who got together and made a spectacle of themselves?

THE ATTACK OF THE BAD JOKES

Coach to the new kid: "OK kid, how high can you jump?"
New kid: "Higher than the Empire State Building."
Coach: "This I gotta see." New kid does a little hop.
Coach: "That's higher than the Empire State Building!?"
New kid: "The Empire State Building can't jump."

A couple of Inuit hunters were in their kayak on a freezing day.
It was so cold so they started a little fire to keep warm, but the
boat caught on fire and quickly sank.
Moral: You can't have your kayak and heat it too.

You: I don't believe in astrology.
Your good friend: You don't?
You: Certainly not. Of course, that's
typical for a Taurus.

I have a very frustrated
pet at home.
It's a turtle that loves
to chase cars.

Two geese were riding through the haunted house.
One of them turned to the other and said "This is
so scary I've got people bumps all over me."

Q: Where do astronauts
leave their spaceships?
A: At parking meteors.

A cannibal family is sitting
at the table finishing up.
The youngest kid comes
rushing in, panting . . .
"Am I too late?"
Dad, picking his teeth,
"Yup. Everyone's already eaten."

Q: How do you keep a
skunk from smelling?
A: Hold its nose.

Q: Where does the king
keep his armies?
A: Up his sleevies.

You: Just by looking at them,
I can tell where you got your shoes.
Your good friend: Where?
You: On your feet.

Did you hear that America plans
to send cows into outer space?
If it works, we'll have the first
herd shot 'round the world.

A couple of backpackers were packing
for a hike through bear country.
One of them was putting in a pair of track shoes.
First hiker: "What do you need those for?
You don't think you can outrun a bear, do you?"
Second hiker: " I don't have to outrun a bear.
All I have to do is outrun you."

Q: Why is it illegal for a man in
Australia to marry his widow's sister?
A: Because he's dead.

Q: What's worse
than finding a worm
in your apple?
A: Half a worm.

Hello, operator? I'd like to
speak to the king of the jungle.
Sorry, sir, but the lion is
busy right now.

Q: What's gray and
stamps out forest fires?
A: Smokey the Elephant.

Q: If a cannibal ate his mother's
sister, what would you call him?
A: An aunt-eater.

A duck walks into a drugstore
and asks for some chapstick.
"Cash or charge?" the druggist asks.
"Oh, just put it on my bill . . ."

Q: What's green, salty and giggles?
A: A dill tickle.

Q: Who wrote Great
Eggspectations?
A: Charles Chickens.

Q: What do you call a clairvoyant
short person who just broke out
of prison?
A: A small medium at large.

Q: What kind of shoes do you
make out of banana peels?
A: Slippers.

WOULD YOU HOLD THIS SQUIRT BOTTLE FOR ME

(AND GET ALL SOAKED IN THE PROCESS)?

A fine piece of outdoor fun. And bonus! It's scientific!

Fill one of those big plastic bottles that soda pop comes in with water. Then take a hammer and nail and drive the nail into the bottle on the side. Pull out the nail and empty the bottle of water.

Next put a small balloon into the bottle and wrap the neck of the balloon around the neck of the bottle.

Fill the balloon with water until it is as full as possible. Then cover the nail hole with your finger and go find a very good friend who's dressed for water sports somewhere outside.

Hand them the bottle and ask them to take a peek inside. As the bottle changes hands, and you remove your finger, the water will come squirting out the top.

As your friend wipes off his or her face, you can explain some of the physics involved . . . how the atmosphere was prevented from getting into the bottle by your finger over the hole. But removing the finger allowed all 33 pounds per square-inch of atmospheric pressure into the bottle where it forced a volume reduction in the balloon. Naturally, the water had to go somewhere . . .

POSSUM WALKING

Ingredients: Two human beings who know and appreciate each other. One has to be a little larger than the other. We'll pretend you're the smaller one.

1 So, you're the smaller kid. Hop onto the bigger person as shown. This is huggie time. The big person has to lock his hands underneath you to keep you in place. Hang onto his neck and wrap your feet all the way around his waist (not hips). Hook your ankles together behind his back. This is key. If you can't lock your ankles together, your legs are too short, or his waist is too big. Sorry.

2 Slowly, carefully, let go of the bigger kid (With your hands! Not your feet!) and fall/lean way over backwards until your hands are on the ground.

The bigger kid has to keep you supported with his hands so you don't go sliding down to the ground.

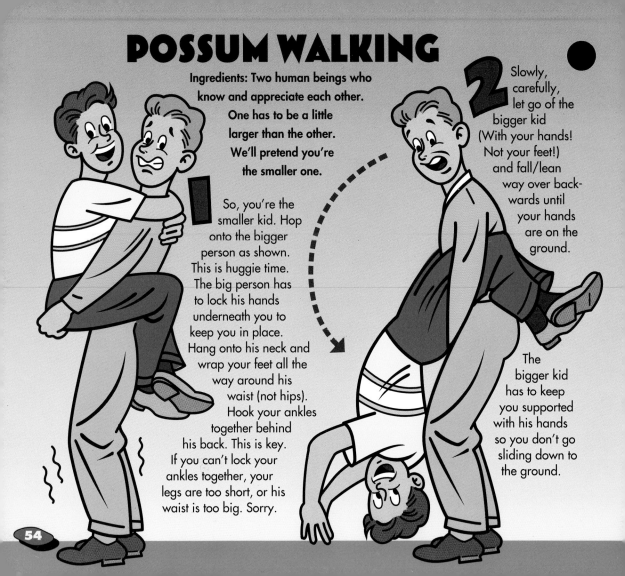

3 Now, handwalk your way back through the other person's spread-apart legs and grab him by the ankles from the back. You are now doing a kind of back arch, so you'd better be a little flexible.

4 Get the bigger person to fall forward onto his hands. Keep your feet locked around his waist. Holler "mush" and off you go, Possum Walking.

Ever at a loss for words when you need to ask someone to step away while you attend to something important . . .? Try these:

Why don't you take a long walk on a short pier?

Make like a tree and leave.

Go tell your mother she's calling you.

You should be on the stage. There's one leaving at noon.

I hope you get ahead in the future. You could use one.

Or maybe you'd like to stop someone from playing the piano . . .? Try these:

Why don't you play "Far, Far Away?"

Why don't you play "By the Window" and I'll help you out?

MUTANTS AND MUNCHKINS

Here's a chance to get those big hairy legs you've always dreamed about. Find a willing hairy-legged grown-up who doesn't mind getting sat upon. Then, step two, sit on him. Put your legs kind of back out of the way and cover both the grown-up and your legs with a blanket or something. Bring in the audience and start in on a couple of hairy-legged jokes or stories. If you have to move about, you can slide around very nicely on "your" bottom if you can get it to cooperate.

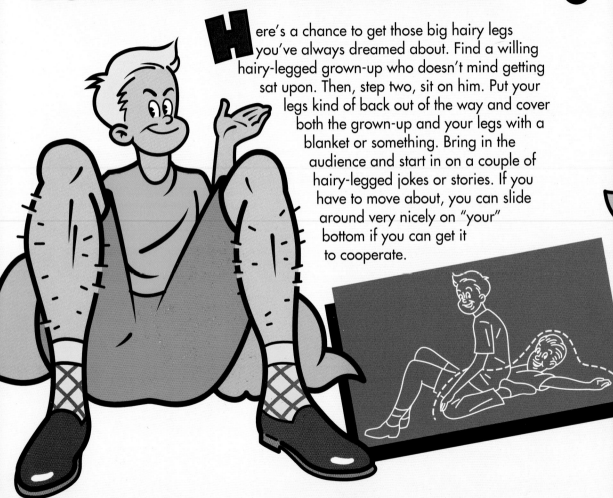

Here's another terrific new way to re-model your whole appearance in a huge hurry. All you need is a willing partner who's wearing something like a loose sweatshirt or jacket, a pair of shoes and a blanket. Oh yes—and a pair of boxers.

Step One: Partner pulls arms out of sweatshirt.

Step Two: You hunker down behind him, get yourself covered with the blanket and reach into partner's empty sweatshirt sleeves (this takes a little personal closeness).

Step Three: Partner puts arms through boxers and into shoes. Maybe get a friend to tidy things up a bit, just to get the appearances correct, and you're all set. You'll look like The Munchkin from Mars. For a quick, cheap thrill, just holler for your parents to come into your room. They will freak out and then rush off for the camera.

But, if you want to do something more than just take a couple of years off your parent's lives, there's enormous potential here. In fact, this little mutation is the basis for what may be <u>The Most Popular Summer Camp Skit of All Time</u>. If you're interested, just turn the page . . .

MUNCHKIN WAKES UP

Perhaps the greatest summer camp skit of all time, this is no-miss, bring-down-the-house, guaranteed entertainment.

Step One: Collect a spoon and a bowl, a box of cereal and a quart of milk. Plus a washcloth, toothbrush and toothpaste.

Step Two: Set up your little monster munchkin on a stool at a table where all this stuff you've collected is set out. (And where a mess is soon to be created).

Step Three: Bring in the audience. Let's say you're the partner whose face is showing. You're supposed to do all the talking, although a couple of comments now and then from your back partner are pretty funny too.

Announce that you've just woken up and are getting ready to do your morning routine. Since "your" hands can't see a thing, you'll have to give them directions for all of what follows.

Q: What's this? ············· A: Worm taking a date to dinner.

It might go something like this:

"*(Big yawn)* Wow! What a great sleep! Guess it's time to wash my face. All I need to do is grab this washcloth that's over to the left there a little bit . . . no . . . a little bit more than that. No. That's too far. Oh yeah. There it is. Now I'll just scrub my face rub-a-dub-dub. Maybe clean out my ears a little too . . . Boy, that feels good. Toothbrushing time! Boy, I sure do love to brush my teeth. My toothbrush is over there to the right. The toothpaste is right here in front of me. No. IN FRONT OF ME! Right, that's it. Now, all I have to do is squeeze the toothpaste onto the toothbrush just like I do every morning . . . real easy . . . not too much . . . NOT TOO MUCH! Then brush my teeth . . . MY TEETH, I SAID, NOT MY NOSE!"

You get the idea. After the tooth-brushing, then it's on to the cereal and all the problems that creates. Take a big bow when you're done.

UPSIDE DOWN FAIRY TALES

Shrimpy Thief Robs Me Blind

by the Giant

Jack was the little criminal's name. I rue the day I ever laid eyes on this vine-climbing varmint.

WANTED

Sometimes you just need a good skit or story idea. Maybe it's talent night, or a slumber party. Or maybe it's just because it's your turn to do a skit or story. But you can't just tell the story of the three bears. Please! Not again! What you CAN do though is take some old stories and turn them around a bit . . .

⭐ Tell the Cinderella story from the nasty sisters' point of view.

⭐ Sleeping Beauty from the witch's point of view.

⭐ Rumplestiltskin's story from old Rumpy's point of view.

⭐ Little Red Riding Hood from the wolf's point of view.

⭐ The Princess and the pea from the pea's point of view.

⭐ Jack and Jill from the pail's point of view.

Try something different . . . How about a baseball game from the ball's point of view; Thanksgiving from the turkey's; Halloween from a pumpkin's . . . ?

Songs of Charm & Childhood

All of the songs that follow have been provided to us by people who have been found to be under 11 years of age. None of these songs have ever been written, read or approved by qualified adults. They have been handed down over the years from kid to kid strictly via the oral tradition.

One Dark Day

One dark day in the middle of the night, two bad boys got up to fight.
Back to back, they faced each other, drew their swords and shot each other.
A deaf policeman heard the noise, and came right out and got those boys.

Great Green Gobs

Great green gobs of greasy grimy gopher guts,
Mutilated monkey meat,
Little dirty birdy feet,
French-fried eyeballs rolling in a pool of glub
And I forgot my spoo-oo-oon!
(slurp)

On the Planet Mars

On the Planet Mars
Where the ladies smoke cigars
Each puff they take
Is enough to kill a snake
When the snakes are dead
They put diamonds in their head.
When the diamonds break
It's the year of '88

We Three Kings

We three kings of Orient are
Tried to smoke a rubber cigar
It was loaded,
It exploded,
Scattering near and far . . .
Oooh
BOOOM!
We two kings of Orient are
(repeat)

USEFUL FOREIGN PHRASES

Here's a collection of handy phrases to use when you're traveling in foreign lands.

English: I am new in your village and would like to know where I might find a restaurant where American rapid food is served.

Farsee: Man Tauzeh bé shahre shoma hastam vá delam meckad bedoonam ke koja Gazayeh Amricayé tond dareen.

English: What a reasonable offer! I shall be happy to pay that much and more, if you like!

French: Quelle offre raisonable! Je serai heureuse de payer autant, et même plus si vous voulez!

English: This dish you're serving me, am I the first to eat it?

Hungarian: Evett már valaki ebböl az ételböl amit nekem kinálsz, vagyen vagyok az elso?

English: Madam, your wolverine has gotten ill on my shoe.

Russian: Madam, vash volchnók vir'val na moi toophel.

English: Excuse me, Mr. Waitperson, may I offer a comment critical of your entree?

Korean: Yoboseyo, yi umsik ae daehaeso pyongka lul naeryo bolgayo?

Q: What's this?

A: Tower of Pisa as seen by a leaning tourist.

IF YOU <u>HAD</u> TO CHANGE YOUR NAME . . .

The following is a list of real names that belong or once belonged to real people. If someone said you had to change your name to one of these, which one would it be?

Make your choice and check your box.
Remember, it's for the rest of your life.

HI, I'M TRULY BORING

- ☐ Ima Hogg
- ☐ Original Bugg
- ☐ Sal Amander
- ☐ Corny Papp
- ☐ Truly Boring
- ☐ Oscar Asparagus
- ☐ Rotten Earp
- ☐ Cherry Pies
- ☐ Young Boozer
- ☐ Buck Tooth
- ☐ Felty Goosehead

- ☐ Flash Dumdum
- ☐ Joanne Floozbonger
- ☐ Orphia Outhouse
- ☐ Kasper Kwak
- ☐ Candy Kane
- ☐ Minzo Nutt
- ☐ Leo Snozzie
- ☐ Doodle Dang Wang
- ☐ Curt Puke
- ☐ Humann Klump
- ☐ Otto Tittlefitz

Not long ago there was a young boy named Falling Rock, who lived on an Indian reservation. He lived there with his family until one day he disappeared. His parents, naturally enough were very concerned. They looked for him everywhere. They started a publicity campaign to get other people to help find him. It wasn't long before posters and signs were up everywhere in the attempt to locate the young man. Some people even put up signs by the side of the road to remind motorists that they should "Watch For Falling Rock."

MORE ACKNOWLEDGEMENTS;

Michael Stroud*
Soozee Shireman*
Martin Gardner
Megan Comfort*
Marilyn Green*
Becca Center
Jodi Kantor
Jay Weisberg
Paul Doherty
Betsy Garties
Keith Gutierrez
Bill Doggett
Davey Burke
Geoff Hoyle
Bill Olson
Joan Burdick
Paul Mabray

*Really special
acknowledgements